MAKING MILLIONS WITH YOUR BUSINESS

How to Start and Grow Your Business

Anthony Chukwuma

MAKING MILLIONS WITH YOUR BUSINESS

Copyright © 2023 by Anthony Chukwuma.

All rights reserved.

No part of this book is for reproduction or imitation in any manner without written permission, except in the case of brief quotations embodied in critical articles or reviews.

All scriptures used in this book are taken from the King James Version of the Bible, except otherwise stated.

Content

DEDICATION

I dedicate this book to the almighty God. I know this sounds like a cliché but if it wasn't for His help, I am sure I may not have started, let alone complete this book.

During the 8 months of embarking on the Journey of writing this book, I felt like giving up a few times for many reasons but seeing it become a reality speaks volume of His encouragement and support through the process.

Secondly, I want to thank you for considering to buy and most importantly read this book and I am hopeful that if a line, a paragraph, a chapter or the entire book helps you – then my job here is done.

And I would like to thank you for giving my words a chance of adding to your amazing journey.

Now get on with it! There is a lot to learn.

Anthony

The Voice

INTRODUCTION

'Experience may not always be the best teacher, but you can pick lessons from experience and know what you must never repeat if you are going to win in business.' – Anthony Chukwuma

Starting a business is exciting. The process of idea creation, role-playing, planning; talking to friends, and making millions in your mind — It can all be really amazing! Sadly though, many people wind up in frustration and bankruptcy despite having that initial adrenaline rush.

I decided to write this book because I thought about you. It's especially yours if you desire to start a business that you believe will make you rich and famous, or perhaps you just admire the 'business owner' title.

With the growing popularity of billionaire entrepreneurs, more people are motivated to become founders, entrepreneurs, and business owners. However, we are hardly taught how to go about it. I would like to help you on this journey. I thought about the costly mistakes you might have made or are prone to make, and how I can help you avoid them.

Helping you to start and sustain a successful business is the crux of this book. It is birthed from real experiences. Business is a journey of growth, profit and loss, and it requires your time, energy and resources. Patterns exist for all records of success. What if I told you that this book can teach you a pattern that will help your business succeed? Well, that's the truth.

Applied knowledge is power. Hop right into this piece of magic, let me help you discover how to thrive in business!

CHAPTER ONE

DO IDEAS TRULY RULE THE WORLD?

In 2015, I implemented a business idea that I thought was God-given. As it is with most of us, it felt like no one else had my 'brilliant' idea. At the time, the closest eatery to where I lived was at least two kilometres away. Even worse, we had access to only one restaurant at my workplace — and their food was a waste of money.

I am a foodie and since it was a problem to get decent food at home and work, I came up with an idea. I wanted to start a food delivery business. Only a few food delivery businesses existed in Nigeria in 2015 and while they operated the regular delivery idea, I wanted to tweak mine a bit. I wanted to give each customer the option of ordering food from multiple restaurants at a time. So with my model, you were supposed to be able to get rice from one restaurant, your favourite chicken from another restaurant, and maybe your preferred type of plantain from yet a different vendor—all in one plate, one order, same delivery fee. For all the guys already in business, you could only purchase from one restaurant per order. So, if you liked their rice and disliked their chicken, you would either just buy or pass—or order your chicken elsewhere and pay delivery fees for each order.

At the time, my idea was amazing to me because it solved my problem. I decided to turn my imaginary business into reality by purchasing two delivery bikes, branding and equipping them for the business, and employing two riders. Undaunted and excited about my business, I threw in the required capital to get it started and within a few days, I started making some money. I named the company BrownBox Deliveries.

Remember that BrownBox was born out of my frustration at not having access to the kind of food I liked. One lesson I have learnt in my years in business is this: not every idea born out of your frustration will sell.

***Not every idea born out of your
frustration will sell.***

Your frustrations are not enough. Ideas that sell
are based on the frustrations of other *people*. If

other people do not have similar frustrations, forget about the idea. The larger your *people* are, the better for you. An exception to this is the luxury goods market where you may need just ten wealthy people to buy only ten bespoke luxury items and the billions roll in.

Your excitement is also not enough. You don't just get excited about an idea and start a business. You must do a survey and test the idea in the marketplace. The marketplace here is the group of people that you intend to showcase your product(s) and eventually sell to. Don't be like me in 2015, ready and excited to run with my frustration as a great idea, without researching the thoughts, opinions and needs of others.

Another major mistake I made was to assume that my neighbours were already my customers. I didn't try to find out how they solved the problem of little or no access to good food. Did they hire a chef? Were they okay with the distasteful food we had access to? Perhaps it wasn't so much of a problem for them as it was for me.

It's unwise to start a business based on excitement, passion, assumptions, or personal frustration without doing thorough research on the demand for your idea in the marketplace. By doing this, you become susceptible to bankruptcy and frustration — as was the case with BrownBox. Eventually, I had to close shop.

I've seen many people create ideas that sound great, but which have little or no demand in their marketplace. The lesson to learn here is this, my friend: ideas are not difficult to come by for many. What determines a great idea is where you are (who you have access to), who you are (how much of your brand you identify with), what you do (how you structure your work), and the unique variation of your idea expression (how you differentiate your offering).

Using BrownBox as a case study, my idea was based on who I was and the circumstances that surrounded my environment. There was no thorough investigation to verify if the problem was a peculiar one or if it affected a hundred more people within my estate or office.

Many entrepreneurs often find a problem to solve without doing adequate research on the weight/significance of the problem in their environment/marketplace. Your idea can only sell as far as the total number of people who have the problem you are addressing/solving and who are looking out for the solution your idea is bringing.

If I had found 200 other individuals in my area in 2015 who had a similar problem with ordering food and needed help as much as I did, an instant 200-person customer base would have made a huge difference in my income. If, on the other hand, I went to one of the busiest streets in town with numerous restaurants within walking distance and tried to execute the same business idea, the business would be dead on arrival because people could easily walk into any of the restaurants to buy the food they desired.

Again, your ideas must constantly revolve around the pain points or desires of your target market. While creating your ideas, you must consider your location, industry, specific area or sector of interest, and target market. A great idea in one location can be useless in another location.

Recently a close friend shared his business idea with me and as he spoke about launching a laundry and dry-cleaning service in the area where we live. I was so sure he was set for a loss. Approximately 80% of the people in the area either had washing machines or maids who helped out with laundry. His idea might have been great in a location with people who had no washing machines or house helps, had money, and were too busy to wash their own clothes. I asked him two questions:

~ How many of your friends do you think would be willing to pay you to dry-clean their clothes?

~ How many machines do you need to get started?

He moped for a bit. It was obvious he hadn't given his idea so much thought. I realised he had walked into a dry-cleaning firm with a little over 100 clothes hanging, estimated the cost of each piece to be within N500 to N1000, and concluded that dry-cleaning companies were cashing out.

Funny enough, I was once just as guilty as my friend. While imagining having my own restaurant as a young entrepreneur, I walked into a restaurant and sat down to run a quick view of things. I calculated the number of tables in the restaurant, the number of meals on the tables, and the number of people there. I could see myself owning a restaurant already! Now that, my dear friend, isn't how to survey a business. You need to know who established the restaurant, why it was established, and the kind of network or circle of friends the owner operates in. It's possible that the owner is well exposed to a huge network and has hundreds of friends and acquaintances who like to eat out; hence, opening a restaurant becomes a good idea.

Moreover, a great idea for one could be a weak idea for another. Always start your journey of implementing an idea by asking the right questions, checking the numbers, weighing your options objectively, knowing the people or tools you need to work with, and where to position your business to win big. As a startup, always think about location. Ensure your idea starts by filling a gap in society or fulfilling the needs of a group first. If it can't fulfil the needs of a group, it can't go national, let alone international.

CHAPTER TWO

HOW TO KNOW THAT YOUR IDEA WILL SELL

'The saying "Ideas rule" isn't completely true. It is sellable ideas that rule.' — Anthony Chukwuma

Perhaps you have an entrepreneurial mindset, constantly buzzing with ideas. Or you are the executor, always ticking boxes and executing ideas. Or you are clueless about ideas, but would support the process of making other people's ideas a success. Whatever spectrum you fall into, I can show you how to vet ideas.

For the past 15 to 20 years, I have been privileged to have tonnes of ideas. I am considered a fast starter by my friends because I am quick to execute the ideas I find worthwhile. However, while quick implementation may sound great, I have learnt some good, yet hard lessons in the process and have had to quit some businesses as well.

As an entrepreneur, you must know the ideas to keep and the ones to quit or you just might find yourself sinking. The heart of idea creation is looking at problems in a way we haven't seen them before. I recently read a quote, 'You stop seeing it as the same, if you look at it differently.' Problems are literally ideas. To start the process of checking if your idea is solid, here are three business test questions to weigh it by:

1 Do you know a *'people'* who would be interested in buying this service or product apart from yourself?
2 Do you understand their frustration and desired solution? Not what you think... what

you have confirmed. (This means you would have to find out from them.) A survey can help you with gathering their thoughts and feedback. It's a goldmine set to help you test or weigh your ideas.

3 Is it a need or a want? A need is anything required to live and function (e.g. food, water, shelter, clothes, etc.) while a want is something that makes you feel good or improves your quality of life (e.g. the latest mobile phone).

In my experience, wants have always made people more money than needs.

You've probably seen people spend more lavishly on what they want than on what they need. Such persons might buy a gadget or phone worth thousands of dollars without hesitation, but bargain strongly in the market when they buy food— owning a shiny new gadget is emotion-based.

Does it now make sense why people spend more on their wants than they do on needs? Make a mental picture of how people haggle over the price of food items in the market versus the ease with which they pay for luxury items. This shows that people spend more on their wants than needs.

I believe that God gives the same idea to many at once. The difference lies in how you build, develop and launch yours. Someone else in another part of the world or within your space is thinking or perhaps already running with the same idea you think is absolutely new. This is why when a great idea comes to you and you fail to act on it, you may be surprised to see the same idea— perhaps highly profitable in another location—being implemented.

Once you have successfully answered the three business test questions, you need to research further. Let's assume you got good feedback from the first survey and believe your idea is loved by many. The next question would be: Can this idea generate money for me now?

This is an important question because an idea being great doesn't necessarily mean it would make you the desired profit now. Example: Imagine that you want to start a business that involves the weekly printing of a two-page publication on investment opportunities in Africa, within an estate of about 700 homes. You carry out your first survey and everyone says it's a brilliant idea, as they would want a bulletin to show them how best to invest and make more money.

Based on research, it could take a week to put together the required publication. How much would anyone want to pay for a two-page publication though? An average newspaper costs N200, so perhaps selling the publication at N100 would be more realistic. (We will discuss pricing in detail later. This is just an assumption for the purpose of this example.) You have to consider the cost of producing 500 to 700 copies at least. Imagine that the cost of production is N60,000 and selling 700 copies would yield N70,000, which is excluding the cost of delivery to all homes. Plus, to be on the safe side, you must consider the unlikelihood of getting 100% sales. It could be a 50% sale in the end.

In this case, you have a great idea but unfortunately, it's one that won't make you any money. This is one of the biggest issues *idea people* face: their ideas are great, but are rarely money spinners.

An honest evaluation of the three business questions will help you determine if your business has the potential to make you money. After you have determined if your idea has the potential to make you money, the next thing to consider is competition. Hence, the next question is this: Is anyone else already doing what I am about to do?

Previously, I mentioned that there is no such thing as a novel idea. Every idea has its expression in some variation somewhere. So find out who is doing what you want to do and how they are doing it, as that would help you to know the competition that exists for your idea in the marketplace. Knowing your competitors would help you know what you need to learn from them and how to better position yourself in the marketplace.

How the marketplace will respond to you and your competitor may be different, especially if you do business in different locations. For instance, if you're in Africa and your competitor is in England, that's a different ball game. You should find competitors in Africa to know the best unique selling point, tweaks or variations to introduce that would appeal more to the market. (Don't dwell so much on this though. It's great to know your competition, but not necessary to allow their outlook affect your decisions. Focus on why they succeed and why they fail.)

At the time of writing this book, I have spent 17 years in the education industry. One of the most successful companies in the industry developed a platform that allows students to apply to over 1,000 universities globally from any part of the world. Other competitors could connect students to only one university at a time and didn't give them a lot of room to make their own choices.

This pacesetter leveraged technology and gave students the power to make their own choices – from a pool of over 1000 universities. Even better, this service was free. They were born at a time when student mobility was popular, yet expensive. They disrupted the market by opening up a world of opportunities to students and making it easy and affordable to gain entry into world-class universities.

When this company was founded, it grew astronomically. After some time, it seemed like they were growing faster than they could manage and soon started to lose their ground. They couldn't handle the number of calls, enquiries and support needed by the students they served. Soon enough, word got out that they were not efficient, and that reputation has stuck for over five years.

Other companies saw the gap and jumped into the market with the same model. They all promised efficiency, the one thing that made the first company lose market share.

Today, these other companies have gained a valuable market share. Based on my estimates, while the first company used to have 80 to 90% of the market share, they may have lost 30 to 40% of that share to competitors.

The moral of this story is this: When you carefully observe your competitors, even though there are slight variations between what they are doing and what you want to do, you will better understand how to enter a market, stay relevant, sustain a valuable drive, and make a difference that will suit the market.

Having studied your competitors, you can now introduce more appealing products and services that are more acceptable in the marketplace than those of your competitors.

What Is Your Unique Selling Point?

To state your USP simply means to state what you're offering differently from your competitors. Some people think it has to be something extravagant, luxurious, or extreme. Well, it only has to be *different*. For instance, it could be that you are delivering on a promise others aren't delivering on.

Some years ago, Domino's Pizza came up with the promise, 'If your pizza is not delivered in 25 minutes, you don't have to pay.' That's a unique selling point and a guarantee. Though it's a promotion-based promise, no other pizza company was doing that at the time; hence, it made them stand out from the others.

I worked with a university in Canada for about two and half years and one of the things we did was to assure all students who applied for a session that even if their visas were not released, we would allow them to start school online while waiting for the visas; also with a guarantee that even if they got a visa denial, we would refund the fees for that semester. Did this work? Absolutely! Students were relaxed and confident enough to pay even when their visas were not yet processed—because of our refund guarantee. And how did this help us? We were sure they would remain our students during the lengthy visa processing period and not change their minds.

Your USP is simply what you would do differently to attract more people to your products or services. Tesla Inc. is an American multinational automotive, artificial intelligence and clean energy company with headquarters in Austin, Texas. They produce electric cars - that is their USP. Your USP can also be a little tweak to a product or service to make it different from the norm.

Another question you should answer when establishing your idea is this: If I remove the core satisfactory promise of this business, what would be left?

Every business has what I call a core satisfactory promise, which is the main incentive you want the idea to achieve for your target market. A good example would be the airlines' promise of conveyance. Despite producing vehicles and their parts, the automotive industry's main promise is also conveyance. The core satisfactory promise of mobile service providers is communication. Educational agencies promise a platform for quality education.

Besides the main promises however, all the service/product providers mentioned here have supplementary benefits that accompany their core satisfactory promises to you. Airlines do not just give you conveyance, but also provide great food, excellent service from air hostesses and sometimes onboard entertainment. Vehicles also come with air conditioning systems, a radio or CD player, and some have massage chairs.

Every idea you establish must have supplementary benefits that would help your customers see beyond your core satisfactory promise. That can be your unique selling point or the feature that endears your customers to your product or service.

In summary to validate if your business idea would make you money you have to:

- Assess the idea using the three business questions
- Check if it is commercially viable – can it make you "real" money. Do some math here!
- Check what area(s) you can deliver better than your competitors
- Identify your Unique Selling Point – what is the extra you will promise your target market

__Business partnership is a risky venture. If you must partner, partner right!__

CHAPTER THREE
HIRING, PARTNERING OR SOLO WORK?

'Business partnership is a risky venture. If you must partner, partner right!' — Anthony Chukwuma

Let's talk risks! The choices you make in a business partnership are risks in their own right. However, there are simple rules to the game. Whether you want to work alone, work with people or have a partner, I have a set of questions that can help you.

In 2018, I started a business that was intended to manufacture and sell beard oils. At the time (and even more as I write this), there was so much hype about men who had beards. That excitement about beards prompted me to jump into the beard oil business. My product was supposed to make beards look radiant and healthy. Some of the questions that flooded my mind as I ventured into the business were: How do I tap into this industry and be a big player in it? What do I do when I run out of the product? (Because I had to rely on a third-party company to make the oil for me to repackage.) What would I do when I decide to create my own beard oil?

Since I didn't know much about the business and had questions on my mind, I decided to contact a cosmetologist and together, we created a masterpiece oil (well, it seemed so at the time).

To get the new and exciting idea started, I met this incredibly creative young man who had also attained success in life and was an excellent business developer with a great understanding of the intricacies of business. Choosing him as a partner seemed perfect because we both had beards, liked business, and wanted to make money. With our healthy, luscious beards in place, we could be the models in marketing the beard oil.

We started a company with 50/50 stakes and worked out the plans and fine detail. In the first few weeks, it was exciting but eventually, the business crashed. In retrospect, I thought to myself: 'How can a creative young man with a great personality and business development and entrepreneurial skills partner with me, yet the business fails?'

I realised that one of the reasons why the business failed was simply divided focus. Even though we were building the company together, we had divided focus. He loved real estate—which I didn't have much interest in—while my passion was education support services. The beard oil business for both of us was just something we wanted to use to generate more money. Our *why* was feeble.

Our intense engagement with other ventures robbed us of the tenacity required for partners to succeed in business. These engagements also meant that we lacked the time to plan and review things together. We would always have to reschedule meetings. Even worse, we both were doing 9-to-5 jobs besides the real estate and education support businesses.

Lastly, decision making was slow. Since we could barely meet to deliberate on issues, decisions were delayed. Many times, my partner would find packaging options he liked and conclude with the designers before I would know about the plan. I would later see it and raise objections, which would make us go back and forth, which further took a toll on the business. Even though we once produced about 100 bottles of beard oil and made at least 100% profit from selling them, our business couldn't thrive.

Here's the lesson in this story: **focus is a major contributor to success, even more than partnership!**

While it's true that the Bible says that one can chase a thousand and two can chase ten thousand (Deuteronomy 32:30 paraphrased), it doesn't validate the assumption that every business owner should have a partner. Many business owners have taken the scripture above to mean that you need to partner to succeed, simply because there's growth in partnership. In business, I want to challenge you to think differently however.

In business, your partnership doesn't have to be with somebody who shares ownership of the company. So, to people who want to get into a partnership that involves owning the company with someone else, I usually suggest this: Consider what this person is bringing to the table. Is it something you can pay for? Can you hire someone who can do it?

These are critical questions to ask before rushing to share a part of your business. Your employee, contractor and consultant are partners too. Try them first before splitting shares.

Imagine that Ethan can build state-of-the-art websites and David is starting a drinks company and perhaps needs a website to sell effectively and reach more people online. Does it make sense to enter a partnership with Ethan that requires splitting the company's shares 50/50 or 40/60, just so that Ethan can build the website for David and maintain it? It might sound like a great idea especially if the business depends highly on technology, till David asks himself: 'Can I pay for tech advice/support rather than having a shareholding partner?'

I don't believe you need to have a partner—a co-owner—when you're starting a small business, it takes more time. The process of starting and maintaining the company is much slower, especially when both parties have unrelated areas of interest and focus. If interests are alike and both persons are 110% ready to build that one business, the business would probably have a better chance at survival.

I'm not against partnering, however. What I am against is partnering for no solid business reason.

The world is fast-paced; hence, if partnering with another would take three days to make a decision that another company will take three seconds to make, you've lost on time and your competitive edge.

One of the first questions you should ask yourself when you're starting a business is *why? Why am I starting this business?* The *why* helps you understand what you have to achieve. It's like a compass, helping you to navigate. And if you know exactly what you want to achieve and figure out how to get there, then *who* you require to get there becomes a lot clearer.

Let's assume you believe you need a partner and have a few candidates in mind. Consider these critical questions before you take that step:

~ Why do you want this partner?

~ Are they bringing in expertise?
~ If they own a part of the business, would they be able to open doors in 10 months that you could only open in 10 years?
~ What exactly are they bringing to the table? State this in detail.
~ Would they be a silent partner who would bring in the money to scale the business but would not participate in the day-to-day running of the business? (This is also a way to partner in business.)

Answering these questions would determine whether you should or shouldn't go ahead with partnering.

On the flip side, you can consider being creative with selecting and appointing partners. As I highlighted earlier, your employees are also your partners. They should be treated as such if you want them to remain in your company for the long haul.

Before I joined one company, the owner and CEO made me a promise. He said, 'Anthony, if you join the company, one of the things I'll do beyond your salary and commissions is that I will give you a percentage share of the company after one year if you meet your target'

Initially, I had no intention of joining, but that one offer changed my mind. It meant that I could co-own this multi-million-dollar firm within a year—even if it was a tiny percentage.

I thought about it and figured if I played my cards right, I would have a percentage of the company. After a while, I understood his strategy. I would work with him for one year, meaning I would be an employee for that period. He would have gotten to know my abilities and how I could contribute. Hence, giving me a small percentage would increase my ownership mentality and keep me by his side. Smart!

This is something I would love small businesses to do. Don't rush to cut a piece of your cake for everyone who comes along. Never do it just because you want them to stay with you or because you think their skills are necessary to run the business. You can get them on board but don't give them a piece of the cake immediately. It's advisable to apply this same tactic my former boss applied and let them work for 12 to 36 months before deciding if what they're bringing to the business is good enough to keep them for the next 20 to 30 years.

Before I get crucified for proposing the idea to not rush into partnership, let me add that the right partnership will move you farther and faster. Your focus should be on determining what type of partnership you should adopt as a startup or small business.

__The vision has to be one so that execution will be fast. It has to be singular so there will be progress and completion will be swift.__

The vision has to be one so that execution will be fast. It has to be singular so there will be progress and completion will be swift. That's one of the things that I have learnt in my business. For a fact, in total, I have founded over 20 businesses. Only about 10% of them are running and doing well currently. The other 90% that failed have one thing in common: I went into diverse partnerships that I didn't have any reason to go into.

One of the core mistakes entrepreneurs make when starting businesses today is to bring in family members as partners, either for sentimental reasons, out of excitement, or perhaps under the guise of wanting the business to stay in the family. A similar mistake is to bring in best friends or random investors in hopes that the investors' money would secure the business financially. Two great questions to answer here are these:

~ Will you need them in 10 to 20 years?

~ Can you employ that talent rather than share stocks with them?

Think long term. Long-term thinking is necessary because the moment you stop needing the person or their expertise, the whole process becomes a drag. It would be late at that time because another person already has a chunk of your business. Friction could set in because the person who owns maybe 40% of your business is no longer relevant to the business' growth.

It's always better to plan with the future in mind. For example, you can create a percentage of shares that you need to give to employees who will eventually become your partners.

I love the model that companies like; PwC and Deloitte adopt. They make their employees partners once the employees have proven to add value to the business and their skills have become key to the success of the firm. They give you a chunk of their business, making it hard for you to under-deliver or leave. The small share percentage does something to the employees' psyche as co-owners.

In summary, when it comes to partnerships that require splitting shares, don't rush! Take your time till you can determine the person's short-term and long-term value. You can always bring in employees or people who believe in your business and decide to work for commissions, which is an advantage to you because you can use their skills. There might also be people who decide to work for a meagre pay because they believe in the business and you offer them a promise to co-own the business in the future.

People buy from those they know, like, and

trust.

CHAPTER FOUR

WHY DO PEOPLE BUY?

***'If people like you, they'll listen to you, but if they trust you, they'll do business with you.'* –
Zig Ziglar**

Countless books exist on why people buy or don't buy, and how men and women buy. Findings and statistics in these areas matter.

There are four major reasons why anyone would buy your product, and the bulk lies on emotions. Emotions have a lot to do with buying—in men and women alike. You might have noticed people go to the market and insist on patronising a particular vendor because of how the vendor related with them in the past. The emotional connection from the previous buying experience would position the vendor as the best in the buyer's mind, not minding the other vendors in the market who probably sell the same commodities at even cheaper prices.

If you understand why people buy, you would be better equipped to position what you're selling.

The Four Reasons People Buy

1. *People buy to ease discomfort*. People will buy a product to alleviate pain. Imagine having to walk for two hours to get to an event, versus ordering an Uber or Bolt to get there in 20 minutes or less. The fear of the pain of walking for two hours would likely prompt you to pay for a ride.

Aversion to pain or suffering makes people buy. This kind of buying tilts more towards needs because the commodities involved are considered essential. Take food for example: if you had none for a long time, you could die of starvation. The fear of the pain of starvation would make you buy food at all cost.

2. *People buy by inspiration*. Businesses promote their products with beautiful female models or handsome, well-dressed, successful-looking men in adverts to stimulate the desire to look, live, and be like

them. People see these adverts and buy out of inspiration. They're motivated to buy because they're inspired to. This is where wants come in.

Why do you think people buy a Bentley for hundreds of thousands of dollars? Inspiration! Even though most of it is informed by wanting to fit into a certain status or standard in society, it's still inspiration.

3. *People buy when they find out (or are made to feel) there's a gap in a particular area.* Some years ago, I stumbled on an advert that so aptly sold how one could make over 6 figures by enhancing their Business analysis skills. I was caught by the Business analysis bug and I felt that I needed to take this course.
I believed that it would increase my capacity to earn a better income and take me to the next level in my career.

Some industries would educate you first (so you know why you need what they're selling) before they get you to buy from them. They show you how what you decide to buy from them will take you to the next level.

Universities do this. They invite you to enroll in their institution by selling the institution as a product you need. For example, they could sell the product thus: 'University A has the best business administration programme and there is a 98% employability guarantee for their graduate students across the world.' The goal of their advert is simply to show you the benefits of having what they are selling to you.

As a business owner, this is important because sometimes you need to take your potential customers to a place of awareness, which in turn would influence their buying behaviour.

4. *People buy to show their status: A set of Cate Blanchett's earrings, bracelet and ring is estimated to cost about 18 million dollars. Madonna's Harry Winston jewel cost about 20 million dollars and Beyonce's Lorraine Schwartz necklace is estimated to cost about 12 million dollars.* What do these all have in common? They are status items.

This type of buying is inspired by the ability to afford an item and because it shows your status.

For some people, buying is a way to inform society that they have attained a certain status and in a bid to prove it, they see the need to drive the latest luxury car, own a private jet, have the latest I-phone, and the list goes on. It's a way to make the statement, 'I can afford it now, I'm making good money'.

Marketing is not the same as selling, and vice versa.

CHAPTER FIVE

HOW TO SELL, PROMOTE OR SCALE YOUR BUSINESS

'No matter how many customers you have, each is an individual. The day you start thinking of them as this amorphous 'collection' and stop thinking of them as people is the day you start going out of business.' – **Dharmesh Shah**

Every small business, as the name implies, starts small. I say this while assuming there is not much money from your business yet. Hence, when it comes to promoting and scaling, you have to be systematic and strategic so you don't run out of money doing these things or competing with the 'big boys'. Before getting into the basics of promoting a small business, know this:

There are two things you must do as a business owner:

1. You must market.

2. You must sell.

Contrary to popular belief (especially in Africa), marketing and sales are different, even though they are connected. If you own a Chinese restaurant for example, marketing is like a wide net thrown to catch hungry men. You could have an ad that says, 'If you're hungry, I know just the right thing for you.' Or 'Click here if you're hungry.'

Selling, on the other hand, is approaching or contacting the hungry men you have found already. In this case, you could say 'The best kind of food to eat to quench your hunger is Chinese food and we have them.'

Do you see the difference? Selling is pointing your target to your products or services. Now, as a startup, what do you have to do? Beyond marketing, you need to position yourself to sell more.

To sell effectively, relationship building is key.

Some years back, I went to a restaurant in Abuja for dinner with my wife. It was the first time we would visit that restaurant. A waiter approached us with the menu, waiting to receive our order. I picked the eleventh item which was pasta. But then, he did something that made me connect with him differently. He leaned towards me with a smile and whispered like he wanted to share a secret: 'Sir, I would recommend that you try item 5'. It was another type of pasta, yet that singular action made me connect with him differently.

I felt an immediate bond and could tell that he cared about me enough to recommend a better dish. Instantly, I asked my wife if we could try the pasta on item 5. And she was open to it, so we ordered. When it was time to get a drink, I called the same waiter to ask what wine he would recommend—because I already felt a connection with him. He recommended different varieties of white and red wine. And yes, I chose from his recommendations because he had built a relationship with me within a few seconds.

Now, this story is meant to reiterate the importance of building a strong relationship with your customers. In sales, building a relationship with your customers is as simple as walking towards a client to connect with him or her from the very first second you meet. Show some interest in their personality: find out their birth dates, interests, their hobbies, the kind of car they drive, the number of kids they have, their hangout spots, etc. A connection can be built within a few seconds, while a relationship can be built in a space of one or two years. Some people don't think they can do this, but the truth is you can if you are willing to give it a try.

Let me also talk about the different personality types in sales. While I initially didn't want to put this in this book, after some thought, I figured that it would be essential to do so. I have dealt with people from all over the world and I have found four interesting personality types you would encounter in sales. You could see two or more of these traits in one person, but there is usually a dominant one.

If you desire to get to know people and learn how you can build a relationship with them, this should interest you. Remember that building a relationship with your clients is non-negotiable if you must grow as a business. Here, you will learn some of the tactics required to build a relationship with each of your buyers' personality types, as well as know how to sell and promote to them. These animal personality types respond to promotions differently—this should interest you.

FOUR ANIMAL PERSONALITY TYPES IN SALES

1. Lion

2. Monkey

3. Dog

4. Fox

LION

Let us do it NOW!

Lions are go-getters.

They want to get things done. If you have ever been in a place where a group of people are given a task, you would see a Lion personality amongst them displaying natural leadership by bringing everyone together to ensure the task is done.

Lions *appear* a bit aggressive, and can be assertive. They are rarely into a lot of detail; they just want to get things done. If you walk into a Lion's office, you would probably see accolades, awards or pictures with people of stature. They like to hang their achievements on the wall. They like to show what they have accomplished. It's just their personality.

If you have the opportunity to sell, say a BMW to a Lion, you might want to focus on selling how efficient the product is, how it would deliver what it has promised; A Lion can resonate with all of that because they want anything that would make them stand out and achieve their goals. So, if you can point a Lion's personality to benefits like an increase in power, recognition and status, you have their attention and interest and have better chances of selling to them.

I used to work with a typical Lion when I was at a UK accounting firm. She had an intimidating personality and if you didn't know her you would think she was trying to overshadow you.

She is one of the nicest and driven individuals I have ever met.

During meetings she had something very "goal oriented" to say. When we had events and something was going wrong, you could visibly see her shake and almost lose it. She had to get things right and deliver beyond expectation – a true Lion!

FOX

Let us make sure its correct/right

Foxes are detail-oriented people.

It is said that Foxes make the best accountants. Have you ever worked in a company where you have to submit a trip expense report to your senior colleague and they say 'Give me two days to review and revert'? You're wondering, *Why two days?* Well, it's because they are detailed and thorough in their approach towards things, people, and life. They're not in a hurry. They can appear suspicious, but that's their personality type.

My wife is a Fox. If I tell her about a business idea, she could take two weeks to research the business, check for reviews on the internet, and more. While I make decisions in 10 seconds, my wife could take three or more days and her favourite lines are 'I am processing it'. Now, that's a typical Fox for you. Foxes take their time to make a buying decision.

So, how can you sell to Foxes? If I am going to sell to a Fox, I must make sure I have my product info, flyers, catalogues, brochures, etc. When I'm leaving their office, I should say something like 'I'm going to send you an email to itemise all that we have discussed. I will also attach our brochure or catalogue to it for your review.' And every one or two days, I would send them more materials or even reviews from other clients. Why? Because that's what makes them buy.

They love data!

Foxes require more detailed information about your brand, product or service before closing a deal with you. They need to understand it; they need to ask a few people about it. Hence, it's in your best interest to approach them with either an e-copy or hard-copy flyers, brochures or other detailed informational material(s) you may have.

MONKEY

Trust me, It's fine.

Monkeys are a fun people.

If you want to meet a Monkey for a sale, they won't mind in a lounge, party, restaurant etc. They are easygoing and excited about the future. Monkeys are very visual too. They see and hear with their eyes more than they do with their ears. You've probably worked in an office where some people are seen as jokers.

Monkeys also love to talk, want to be involved in decisions and also very optimistic

When it comes to buying – peer pressure does affect them and if you can demonstrate that others like them or people they respects are buying, you most likely would sell.

Because they have a strong desire to be liked and find it hard to say NO, they are the easiest to sell to in my opinion. If you want to make a sell to a Monkey – make it easy. Build a relationship, become friends and genuinely care and you will sell.

I am a typical Monkey. I once encountered a salesman who was supposed to sell a house to me. He probably noticed I was a Monkey and just left selling to talk about me. We talked about my family, the house I lived in, how I bought it, my workplace, etc. We laughed about a few things, connected well, built a relationship and eventually, he made the sale.

The tactic for selling to a Monkey is to feed their eyes. Give Monkeys pictures and videos of what you want them to buy. For instance, if you are into educational selling, you want to give them visuals about the university and feed them with entertaining information as well—things that would excite them and stimulate their buying senses. You must show them exciting things. If you want to engage a Monkey with a task, you must tell them the fun part because they resonate with fun. For instance, if I want a Monkey to join me for a road show, I would tell the Monkey that we are going to do a three-hour road show and afterwards, we would jump into Sheraton Hotel and have the best treat ever.

It's the same thing with buying for them. Add a bit of fun to it. If you sell cars and a Monkey comes into your showroom, please give them a drink if you can. Make them feel relaxed. Tell some jokes if possible. The idea is to get them to relax, as that's how they buy.

DOGS

Let us co-exist and keep things stable.

Dogs are caring beings.

They are ever showing care. Dogs are often thinking of how best they can support their family, friends and loved ones. They have a deep need to please others. They can be great listeners and probably give the best advice and encouragement but have a problem with being decisive when it comes to their turf.

If I wanted to sell to a Dog, I would focus on how the product would support them better, as well as help them to make the lives of their family, friends and loved ones easy.

With their indecisiveness you may need to put extra effort to show them why they should buy.

You don't have to go into details about the product, but you must make them see how the product benefits their loved ones, because they are empathetic and are always looking out for things that can help them support the people in their world. With the Dogs, you are selling to others through them.

Dogs will usually have few but deep friendships – if you can get to their friends, you probably would make a sale.

While I can share a lot more about these personalities, I want you to think through each personality carefully. Remember that more than one personality trait can be found in an individual. However, there is usually a dominant one that truly guides how they buy more often. Knowing these animal personality types would better help you to sell and promote to your clients as well as build a long-term relationship with them.

KEY ELEMENTS OF PROMOTING YOUR PRODUCT/SERVICE VIA CONTENT MARKETING

As a small business, to promote right and get the right impact for the promotion, whether via social media or traditional media, you need to consider the following:

Headline

I prefer to call this my marketing line. It's the opening statement or question that captures the attention of my target market or audience. For instance, I work with a university in Canada and if I want to gain my audience's attention, I don't say 'Do you want to relocate to Canada?' Rather I say, 'Are you looking to live, study, work and eventually get your permanent residency in Canada?' Why? It's because I know that people are not just about studying for the fun of it. They have their desires; hence, I created a line or hook to get the attention of a larger number of people.

You must consider this alongside the other glitz and glam like the design.

Unique Selling Point

Take a deeper look at the product. While this second step is not something I do all the time, it's important to know how it works so as not to lose people. The second line after the first marketing line stated above can be 'You can do this through university A, B, C or D'. And perhaps add the uniqueness of the MBA programme offered in the university. I could say 'And you can achieve this through the award-winning MBA programme at the University of ABC.' Or 'In 2022, University ABC won the award for the university with the best MBA programme, which can also help you live, study and work in Canada.' This is a unique selling point to arouse more interest in your audience.

Guarantee

The third thing to note as significant is giving a guarantee. Perhaps you've heard stuff like 'You can purchase our product and if you don't get all it promises within 30 days, then we would ensure 100% money back.' These are guarantees. The truth about this is that people hardly take the guarantees, so never be afraid to give a guarantee. I once read that less than 1% of the people who read your guarantee request for it. Hence, it's okay to always use a guarantee. A guarantee can be many things. It can be refunds, time based, or anything.

A word of caution though, even though people hardly request for guarantees, it doesn't mean you don't deliver on them. Keep your promises.

Few years ago I bought a VR set. I bought some games online with a guarantee that if I played for less than 30hrs and didn't like it, I could return for a full refund. I have bought over 20 games, but have only requested for a refund for one game.

At the time of writing this book, there is a university in the UK, lets call it University of T. One of their powerful guarantees is this: 'After studying with us, if you don't get a job in nine months, we will ensure a full refund of your tuition.' This is because they are confident that you would get a job, but what that guarantee doesn't say is the kind of job or pay you would get. But they are convinced that they would be able to help you to get a job nonetheless.

Create a Sense of Urgency

Always state a limit. *There are only 20 seats available in this seminar*, for example. *Limited scholarship is available*, in the case of a university. The limits you place in your offer are to create a sense of urgency that would cause people to buy into your offer without delay. It doesn't matter the product you are selling, you can create a sense of urgency. You can even put a discount to it by saying 'the first 10 or 20 persons who purchase it would get it at XYZ price, after which the price increases'. Establishing urgency hastens sales, which is what you stand to achieve with this.

Call to Action

This is where so many businesses miss it. They promote, they sell their offer, but they don't tell people where or how to buy. You must state the call to action. The onus is on you to convince them to buy into your offer with a call to action: 'Click here to buy now,' 'Click here to learn more', or 'Are you interested in this? Click here to pay now'. Your call to action could be either direct or indirect. Either way, people must be given the next line of action always.

Contact

It's necessary to give a contact that people can reach you on, after you have shared your offer. You can share your email, phone number, or a social media contact. Share a contact detail that people can easily reach or share with others.

PRICING

Apart from the other techniques I have mentioned in promotion and scaling your business, I have seen people use pricing as a way of getting noticed. It's either they make freebies available or they give out their products or services at low prices to beat their competitors. While this has become a rampant method amongst small businesses, I must say I do not subscribe to this method because there is a difference between a product being cheap and affordable.

A pack of 900 grams of powdered milk can cost about $30 which may be considered expensive by some. To make this affordable, smaller sachets of 50grams are sold at about $2. If you really calculate it you would find out that buying the affordable 50gram sachets eventually becomes more expensive.

18 sachets of the 50grams make 900 grams, however, it would cost you $36 dollars to get the same quantity.

In this case, the product was made more affordable but not cheaper.

Try making your product more affordable first before making it cheaper.

Consider this: The clothes you are wearing, were they necessarily the cheapest at the time you bought them? Rather than make your product the cheapest, you should look for ways to make it affordable first. People often buy the most affordable and not necessarily the cheapest.

There are different ways to get your product to attract people:

1. Affordability
2. Pricing (a discount after a certain number of purchases.)

Now, you can motivate people with discounts in smart ways. There is a coffee shop in the UK that gives you a coupon that needs to be marked out four times to get a free cup of coffee. This tells you that you need to make a four-time purchase to get a free cup. If you go to this shop and they mark out one, when you are done with the coffee, they ask you, 'Did you enjoy it?' When you say yes, they say 'For the good review, we will mark out another for you, so you only need to make a purchase of two more cups to get a free cup of coffee.' The customer feels great about this and would be glad to complete the coffee journey. The catch is that the coffee shop originally intended to give you a coupon for three ticks to get a free cup of coffee.

So, you see? You have to be smart about your pricing. Use pricing technique well. Cheaper doesn't always mean affordable. I don't recommend making your product cheaper to get the attention of your target market. Be wise!

...Success is not a resting place— it is a
launching pad. – Denis Waitley

CHAPTER SIX

COMPETITION AND WHY IT MATTERS

Competition is imperative in business because there is hardly any business idea that hasn't been executed already, even if it's just a variation of it. Think about this. Do you think Amazon was the first to consider selling online? That's unlikely. Someone must have tried it before, but maybe to serve only their immediate community. Consider Facebook too, do you think it was the first online communication attempt? I doubt so. My point is, for every business you want to do, there is someone already doing the same thing or a variation of it.

One of the things I'll like you to do when you have an idea or an existing business is to think of two types of people or organisations, the first being your direct competitors. These are people who target the same people you target, with a product very similar to yours. The second set of people to identify are your indirect competitors.

These are people or organisations that have the same target audience as you do, but with a completely different product. For example, you sell apples on your street and opposite you is a shop that sells meat pies. When a hungry person walks by, they can either decide to buy your apples or the meat pie. This shop is your indirect competitor.

Direct competitors: same/similar product, same target market.

Indirect competitors: different product, same target market.

If a company who has a similar product to yours is targeting a different market, they are not your competitor. For example, you sell shoes targeted at women in their 20s and another brand sells shoes targeted at women in their 50s, they are not your competitor.

After identifying about two to three competitors in your space, find each competitor's unique selling proposition (USP). Every product or service has a USP, which is what makes a brand or product stand out. A USP can be an idea or positioning. For instance, I am about to launch an educational platform that pays students for applying to schools, which simply means rewarding them for choosing to increase their knowledge. At the time of writing this book, there isn't any company in the industry that does that. In launching this product, the fact that it's the first of its kind will be my USP.

It's important to know the USP of your competitors. Some may argue that it's a waste of time to focus on your competitors, but you cannot be the best standing alone—you have to be the best amongst others.

When it comes to knowing about your competitors, the first step is to make sure you are different from them in one way or another, and not trying to become them. There is something you have that your competitors do not have, and that's what makes you stand out. For example, DHL has claimed to be the most networked courier service and hence the fastest. What this means is that another courier service cannot suddenly declare the same. DHL has worked well to earn that USP. Other companies have to find their own footing and forte.

While I stand for brand authenticity, I don't discourage copying. I believe there are no new or original ideas—we only have variations. If you see something amazing and attractive that your competitor is doing, which would add value to your target, copy. Copying isn't bad; it's losing your identity in the process that is. Your originality should remain with additions or features that can further add value to your product. Always remember though, that you should never copy or adopt what you cannot deliver or sustain. For instance, if you are just starting your courier business, you cannot promise worldwide delivery like DHL does, because that's not feasible.

When you consider your competitors, you are learning and examining sustainable features that you can adopt. You're seeking to improve your product while maintaining your uniqueness.

Another key thing is to learn from the mistakes of your competitors. Consider their areas of failure and lapses in delivery which have caused the target market to not really appreciate their product. This is important if you must avoid what your target market detests in your competitors, especially if they are in the same geographical location as you.

You want to know what has made them suffer in the past, so it doesn't repeat itself with your product. That way, you know what promises you should make and when you make such promises, you must deliver.

It's also based on your competitors' mistakes that you can build guarantees for your product, which are statements or tag lines that offer promises to your target market. In essence, you're learning from their mistakes and making corrections in your product.

Competitors are essential to the growth of your business and you should listen to them every now and then. You must know at all times what the market is saying, and what your competitors are doing as well. You must never be in the dark regarding these things. Your target market is like a human being with many potential lovers. If you want to win that person over, you must know what other potential lovers are doing so you can do better. Your aim as a business owner is to make sure your target market always looks at you.

There's a concept I got from the book, Blue Ocean Strategy. It says, 'In the playing field, be very different that you're almost not competing because you stand out'. That's simply explaining the importance of a USP, but you can't have that if you don't know what your competitors are offering your target market. You must know what they're doing to win the market, so you can do it better. Also, think about how much time and resources you can save just by being informed on how to avoid their lapses. It may have taken your competitors months or years to discover some likes and dislikes of the target market but by just learning from them, you're meeting up and walking at the same pace as they are.

In developing your USP, you can add a tangible physical feature, or a service perk like being the first to offer 24-hour service. For example, you may not be the first in the industry, but you can be the first to offer a particular perk in addition to your product. You could also be totally different like Apple. Before the advent of their brand, most phones were black or dark-coloured but they came boldly with a white phone. That is what it means to stand out.

Remember that just as you would pursue a lover, your target market is also your lover. You need to woo them. When they come across your brand, make them take another look. Be different from every other brand they see.

CHAPTER SEVEN

STAY FOCUSED AND FLEXIBLE

'By staying focused and flexible, you will meet and exceed your major life-forming goals. Success is not a resting place—it is a launching pad.' – Denis Waitley

People have come to me several times to say, 'I've got this business idea. What do you think about it?' You know, billions of ideas go around. One thing I always say regarding this is, whatever idea you have, no matter how novel and amazing you think it is, I can bet that 200,000 other people have that same idea or line of thought. The difference between you and the rest is who does it faster and more accurately. Moving and taking action are the actual game changers. That's why I like the Nike slogan, *Just Do It!*

I've discovered that these people who come to me are visionaries. They see something ahead that propels them to take action. People who come up with ideas are sometimes not even the ones to take the ideas the whole nine yards— because they're not execution experts. Some people have a specialty in execution. It's difficult in my experience to find a visionary who is also an execution expert. That's why many visionaries will need other people to execute. These other people have the execution expertise, so all the visionaries have to do is tell them the idea.

Whether you're a visionary or an execution expert, this chapter is for you, even more for the visionaries. Visionaries love their ideas so much that no matter what you say, they're not going to change course. They love and believe so much in their ideas that it's hard to leave room for major changes.

But this is noteworthy: not all great ideas are commercially viable ideas. Not all great ideas can or will make you money. They can be amazing ideas because they have never been implemented or even because they solve unique problems, but they may not make you money. This is where a little tweak can become necessary— a bit of attention to the trends, or the use of technology. Basic tweaks can increase the potential of an idea generating millions for you. Let me give you some examples of companies who tweaked and changed to meet what their target market was demanding of them.

You've perhaps heard about Nintendo, known today for the Nintendo Gaming System and considered a gaming giant. They had started as just a card-playing company. But in the year 1978, they started to develop arcade video game systems. In 1985, they decided to produce game consoles like Donkey Kong and Super Mario. This is just to emphasise that they didn't start with what they ended up with, yet they became champions.

Another company with a similar storyline is Xerox and their photocopying machines. They started out as Haloid Company and their name change happened in 1961. They sold photography paper only. It was many years later they developed photocopying using a technology called xerography; hence, the reason for changing their company name. As the company grew and the Xerox machine became popular, they became Xerox Corporation, as they're known at the time of writing this book.

Not all great ideas can or will make you money.

LG didn't start out selling TV and electronics either. They were a South Korean hygiene and cosmetic products company that only adopted the LG name because they wanted to compete in the Western world. That's when they also adopted the slogan *Life's good.* It was much later they switched fully to electronics.

How about the company called Gap, which makes jeans now, but didn't start that way? Gap started as a record company, but they sold jeans in their outlets. Today, you wouldn't find any record there at all. They now stand as a billion-dollar business that makes nothing but jeans!

The idea behind narrating the stories of these companies is that they've been around for decades but not because of the initial idea of their respective founders. I'm sure the people who came up with the first idea that they ran expected that their idea would make them millions, but were flexible enough to change. Similarly, you have to be open to adjustments and tweaks as a visionary, a company owner, or an entrepreneur. The original idea you had might change depending on what's going on, but that shouldn't be so much of a problem. That change might just be what you and your company needs.

WHAT ARE THE CHANGES THAT THEY MADE?

For some like Nintendo, it was technological development. For others, it was discovering a better niche, like the Gap company that sold records and a few jeans, but soon found out that jeans were the thing to sell.

The bottom line is that to grow as a company, you must listen to the times you are in and listen to the customers you're selling to, and what they're doing and resonating with. You see, your idea is important, but what is more important is the market you are selling to. This means that if the market changes its behaviour, then you need to change your product or service to fit the market you're targeting.

You see, your idea is important, but what is more important is the market you are selling to.

Now, changing lanes is probably one of the hardest things for an entrepreneur to do, because they believe so much in their ideas. But change is necessary. Refusing to change is almost like saying 'If it's not ABC, then I'm shutting down this company'.

I'm not saying all companies must go through such changes, but I want you to have an open mind that this could be the case for you. Personally, I have done a lot of businesses and I have seen companies introduce different technological advancements or different things to shift their product line as well.

I used to work for a company that provided insurance for smallholder farmers in different countries in Africa. Over time, they started gathering data about African farmers and then gradually shifted from being just an insurance broker to a crop information provider because they had so much information about the kind of crops, farmers, locations that are disaster prone and so on.

For the mere fact that they had data, they became so rich and so vast that they now position themselves as a company that sells data. If a company is interested in investing in agriculture in Africa, they would come to them and make enquiries. *'We would like to plant rice. Where is the best location?'* And for every piece of advice they gave or for their consultancy services, a fee was attached. This company didn't shut down; they only tweaked the business a bit because they noticed a gap. And they didn't have to stop delivering their core service – insurance brokerage.

In building a business, staying focused is important, but being flexible enough to adopt new strategies and adapt to your market demands is equally as important.

You must be at a place where you are open to knowing everything happening with your target market and environment. You need to watch out and listen for it, and that's why it's important to also keep an ear on the ground for what's happening amongst your competitors: what's going on, who they are, what they do, and what they're looking at doing.

A few years back, the United Kingdom stopped international students from having what they call postgraduate work. Suddenly the move for international students from Africa to the UK dropped drastically, and everybody focused on Canada because Canada had that option.

Many people in the edtech industry were UK-focused and didn't want to move, but all that happened was that they lost the market. One edtech giant at the time, focused solely on UK schools. However, as this move happened and UK markets started to close, they changed their name. That was how they opened up their doors to other locations, Canada especially. This is what I mean by adapting to what the market is saying. (You must do this to survive as a business.) If the UK didn't open its borders again for postgraduate work permits for their international students, the company would probably have folded.

The Nokia 3310 for example was a miracle. People loved it. It was probably the most bought phone in the history of phones at the time, but they're almost non-existent now. One of the things the CEO said then (paraphrased) was that they were not fast enough to hear the market and change.

These are some of the things entrepreneurs must have in mind so they're able to survive. I always like to say this: 'Consider your market as an individual. See your entire target market as an individual—a beautiful lady or handsome man— and let your task be to continue to woo this lady or guy and have their attention constantly without taking them for granted.'

Do not think your target market is yours forever. Using my analogy, do not think to yourself, *'Now I have this beautiful lady or handsome guy and we are married. It is sealed'*. No market will be yours forever. You have to continue to keep them by giving them all your attention. Let them keep testing your products and services, but it's never a done deal. Don't assume that they're now loyal to you because you offer something that they don't have. Every entrepreneur ought to have this knowledge: be able to adopt new strategies and adapt to the market you are serving.

As a startup, you don't have time or resources to waste, so the more you know before you start, the better.

Consider your market as an individual.

CHAPTER EIGHT

KNOWING WHEN TO DROP AN IDEA: THE HARDEST STRUGGLE OF A VISIONARY ENTREPRENEUR

'As a startup, you don't have time or resources to waste, so the more you know before you

start, the better for you and your business.' –
Anthony Chukwuma

This chapter is probably the hardest for me to write because it's a hard truth. I am a visionary. I am a pure visionary, I don't like to kill ideas. I like to iterate them, change something, tweak it here or there. There are certain ideas that people have discussed with me and I immediately know that it's not an idea they should run with. Truly, it's hard to say to someone who must have brooded over an idea for a long time and planned it out, 'Hey, this isn't going to work!'

A while ago, a close friend of mine came to ask for a loan to start a stationery sales business. He wanted to rent a shop to stock and resell stationeries. He told me about the profit margin he could earn on printers and ink cartridges, and it looked really great at first until I started asking "real" questions – the type of questions entrepreneurs sometimes ignore because of the excitement that comes from starting a business.

My questions revealed that the shop was in the middle of nowhere. No one was going to drive such a far distance to purchase stationeries when they had closer alternatives. That wasn't all.

He couldn't identify one person in his circle who would be a potential customer.

I will not bore you with all my findings, but let me say that this idea of his didn't add up.

I simply told him to abort the idea!

An entrepreneur doesn't have an easy life. You could nurse an idea for months, only for another more experienced entrepreneur to tell you the tough truth that it won't work. This is why every idea must be evaluated early before it is launched.

There are three ways I suggest that you test your idea. If one of them fails, then I need you to step back and rethink the idea. You might just need to tweak something. But if it fails in all the three ways, abort mission!

1. ***The 60% Rule***: This is the first important way to evaluate your idea. The 60% rule is subjective and it simply says you should have done the planning, checked the location, thought around the process of starting the business, and have just about 60% clarity of how the business will go.

Uncertainties exist, so 100% clarity and visibility can be near impossible — just have 60%.

Be able to say 'I know how this is going to play out. I've done my math and if I sold X with a 10% margin, I'll be making a profit and be able to pay my staff. 60% of this product will serve 60% of this certain kind of market. This is how we reach them; this is where they stay. 60% of my target market is on this age range. They read articles on Instagram, so this is how I'll promote. 60% of my target market would love this exact colour.

If you know just 60% of these things, it still means there are certain things you don't understand or have any certainty about, which is fairly fine. If you don't know up to 60% however, I need you to hit the brakes a little.

Always consider what your future competitors with that idea in business are doing. Try to learn from them while you prepare. This can save you great time, money, and effort.

2. ***Know your target market***: This is the second step in determining if it's time to drop an idea or if running with it is worth your time. Your target market is like your potential lover or someone you're chasing constantly to win their heart. They're important because they are the reason you would be in business or not. You would need to get accurate, specific and profound evidence that your product has or can have a huge demand—and the way you get your answer is from your target market.

You need to have evidence that your target market will not just buy your product, but will buy it at the price you set. This is something you must be able to test with people around you. So before you even launch any idea, try the product and sell it at the price you want to sell it. See what the response is like and get feedback that is if your target market can pay the right price for the product. Also, would you be able to reach this target market? Would you be able to penetrate the target market and achieve the profitability goals that you set for yourself? What would you be able to do for your target market? Your product or service must be extremely clear and must add value to your customers.

Consider what happens when you're unsure about these details or when they're unable to pay the right price. All ideas may be interesting even to the point where they're considered great ideas but they may not be commercially viable.

3. ***Find yourself a devil's advocate***: This is a bit different and I'll explain. Find yourself an outsider, especially a dispassionate one; somebody who's not connected to you at all. This person should have no interest whatsoever in making you feel good. As an entrepreneur, because our brains are wired not to quit or give up, it's not so easy to receive the information that your idea isn't that good, especially from a close friend. That's why you need an outsider.

A quick disclaimer here: if you have an idea, many people won't see the depth of your idea because it's unique to you and your space. Hence, you may find them saying it's a bad idea.

The idea originator is usually blinded by the success or hope of success of an idea to the extent that sometimes they don't see the flaws that could be fatal. This is why it's necessary that you talk to someone smart enough, who happens to also be a visionary; someone who can see the way you see, but is also dispassionate.

When testing out your pricing with your target market, be careful to do so across people of different economic realities. That your uncle paid for something to support you doesn't mean they would pay that much to buy from a total stranger. Try other people in your circle who are not as close and see how they respond to your pricing, your product, your quality, the size and the colour, and you'd have been true to yourself about this.

Maintain the same level of excellence in your output, regardless of your current potential client.

If your product fails the 60% rule, you're not sure of the target market and there's a dispassionate outsider who can point out the flaws, drop the idea and move on to the next one. You have to be open enough to know that this can happen or that you may need to change something so that the idea would work. And finally, whatever you do, don't waste time.

CHAPTER NINE

THE SECRETS OF GROWING YOUR BUSINESS IN AFRICA

'Absolute excellence to every man at every time is one true secret to succeeding in your business.' – Anthony Chukwuma

Secret #1

I read a post by Simon Sinek a while ago and he said something really interesting. He said 'There may be patterns for the things that succeed but that doesn't mean there is a formula for success'.

How true! There are patterns for your business to succeed but ultimately, there is no formula that will concretise success. Patterns and formulas are different concepts. A child who goes to school every day, doesn't miss a class, listens to his teachers and does all his assignments has a pattern. That child will very likely be successful when he takes the final exams.

However, that's not a formula for passing exams because there are kids who follow the same pattern yet don't pass. Now, between who passes and who fails, there are other factors at play. One may be that student A has a more photographic memory and a learning style well fitted to how his teacher teaches.

External factors will always be at play—in business and other walks of life. I honestly would rather stick to the patterns because the patterns show indicators that you're doing the right thing. This, however, doesn't downplay the importance of paying attention to external factors. In business, listen to who you are, what you're selling and who your customers are, because those are the external factors that will determine whether those patterns will lead you to your own success or not.

In business for instance, one of the things that everybody says is to make sure your plan is right. Even though planning has been identified as one ingredient that can lead you to success in business, it doesn't mean that if you plan, you will succeed. It's a key ingredient in the pattern that leads to success, but there's no formula anywhere that once you plan, you'll succeed.

There are secrets behind certain successes that are beyond patterns. You have to listen to your external factors and environment to ensure you do what you ought to do, however, you must know that while external factors may lead you to success, they're not the only requirements. There is a peculiarity to these things: your geographical location, your target region, your climate, your upbringing, and the people who surround you. All these can equally affect your business success.

Excellence, for me, is top of the list of what should be adopted as a pattern. Let's assume you're a chef. What is the highest standard you deliver as a chef? Now assuming the President of the United States of America has come into your country to spend three nights and would like for you to make dinner for him and his entourage. My question to you is simple and I need you to think about it well: Is the level of excellence you would put into making them dinner the same as the level you are putting in currently?

Let's take another example. Let's say you're a public speaker and you found out that you're going to give a speech to a group of intellectuals such as professors from Harvard accompanied by the Prime Minister of the UK. Would you take more hours preparing that speech compared to if you were going to speak to secondary school students?

The difference is in the effort and that effort you put into preparing because of a bigger, more advanced and more quality audience is what I call excellence. If you can apply that level of detail, input, planning and quality all the time, you set yourself apart. This is the biggest secret/growth pattern to successful businesses or brands.

Never change your level of excellence simply because you assume the people of a higher calibre will give you more opportunities if you do it better for them than you do for others.

This is one of the biggest problems we have in Africa—lack of excellence. We rarely see people putting in a lot of effort in their businesses to make that product, service or brand stand out.

A while ago, I was having a conversation with my wife and we were talking about why the African community is so attracted to Western services and products.

If you had a product or a service that was made in Africa, especially West Africa, and you position that product or service as coming from the US or the UK, it very likely will sell more. Sadly, even though we're trying to promote the products made in Africa, they're still not equated with products made from the Western countries. People genuinely would value an African product well if a *Made in the UK* was slapped on it.

The reason is not vague at all. It's because people have realised that products from the Western world are usually superior. And it all boils down to excellence in delivery of products and services.

The thing with excellence is that it's a journey, not a destination. Always have that in mind. Whatever it is that you've built today, you have an opportunity to keep improving on it every day, every week, every year, every decade and possibly every century. Just keep improving. Make it better, more accessible, and valuable. Keep bringing more quality into the mix of that product or service. Be detailed, maintain high quality and good standards.

Secret #2

Success boils down to having an excellent product but even more important sometimes, is allowing people to see how good your product is. To get this done, you have to use channels and mediums and platforms that will help you stand out.

You have to be accessible. It doesn't matter how good the product you sell is. If I, as part of your target market, do not know how to get it or I can't reach you, you've missed a customer.

Social media is such an amazing tool for a small business because it's almost free to advertise there. Hence, make sure you're accessible. Find ways for people to know what you do. Post it!

I have been in the education industry for over a decade now, and I always make posts about what I do. I've got friends who never said anything to me, who never bought from me or required my service until after six years. *'Anthony, I remember. You are doing X, huh? I have a cousin who would like to use your service. Do you still have access to it?'* They have known me for six years or more, and they reached out to me after all that time. Why? Because I constantly put what I do in their faces.

I remind them through my posts that I am in X industry, and I have XYZ product or service.

You have to be accessible and one way to do that is to use your social media platforms effectively.

Secret #3

Another thing I would like to say, more like a warning, is to make sure your idea can be commercialised efficiently. Like I mentioned before, not all great ideas are profitable ideas. So you need to figure out how to make sure it can be commercialised. Easy! Try to sell it within your circle at a price that will make you a profit, and see what happens. There are some products with a 2% profit margin while some may have profit margins of 100%.

Hence, the next questions are:

~ Do you know your profit margin?
~ How much are you going to make?
~ At what price will people be comfortable enough to buy that product that would allow you to make enough money to sustain the business?

Secret #4

Don't stop reinventing yourself, your product, and your service. And I boldly want to say copy, remix, and tweak samples from the best ideas that are close to what you're doing or even not so close to what you're doing. I know a lot of people have been sold this theory of *'Hey, do not copy the original'*. And I always say, tell me any original business and I'll call out another business that is a direct copy or an alternative to that business.

Give me any business that was never thought of and is now invented, and I'll tell you how two or three other ideas came together to make that one. So, in my school of thought, there's no absolute original idea or business. Some are amalgamations of different ideas set in diverse creative ways that soon become original copies.

I could have a business that produces bags and I know how to produce wonderful bags, but I see another business that produces toothbrushes and I see how they distribute the toothbrushes. I can copy their distribution plan and strategy, then apply it to my bag business. So even though they are completely a different business, I have been able to copy something that would help my business.

So, don't stop reinventing. Boldly copy, remix and tweak as long as you know it's going to add value to your business. I always tell entrepreneurs that it's not about copying anything you see, but it's more about how effectively you copy, tweak and personalise what you have copied. That is what makes the difference.

Forget about people saying you're doing it like company XY. Yes, do it like XY, but more effectively because when you copy, you get to remix that copy and make it even better.

Secret #5

Think bigger! African entrepreneurs always think about their community alone. I once heard an unconfirmed story about Ford Motors and how they planned the design of their vehicles and how they would ship to the rest of the world, 30 years in advance. How remarkable!

We African entrepreneurs always think too small. We want to just affect our community. While this is a fantastic way to start, we need something bigger than our community. Many businesses in Africa think about how to serve Lagos or Accra, but we do not think about how our products can be beneficial to Asia, down to the USA or the UK.

We need to think bigger. And in thinking bigger, we will find that it does something to the level of detail and excellence we put into our products because of the consciousness that the products aren't just for Africans alone, but for the world. Fortunately, because of social media and how global the world has become, selling to another country is a whole lot easier. So, the idea is to think more than we currently do.

In summary, a solid plan must be in place on how you'll go from one step to another in executing your goals and commercialising your idea. Answering these questions should guide you:

~How much is it going to cost?
~ What is the selling price and cost price?
~ What is my profit margin?
~ Who do I need to make this idea work?
~ Where do I sell it?
~ Who is my target market?

You also have to put all these things down on paper. It's not okay to just think about them. Usually when you write stuff down, you are concretising it in your subconscious, and it would be much easier to see mistakes and loopholes. Once it's on paper, discuss it with friends and family. Let them throw spanners in your wheels. And then be proactive in plugging the loopholes, developing effective solutions and problem-solving strategies.

In all, let the following remain top of mind as a business person in Africa: to grow, to be seen, and to be recognized globally. Let entrepreneurship in Africa challenge you to step out and be different.

CONCLUSION

I've been around long enough to know I could tell you 200 ways to be successful in business. For you however, maybe only one would work. And this is because there are a lot more pertinent factors than what you have read in books. Also, I don't know who you are. I don't know how you learn, how you adapt or how flexible you can be. I don't know your target market or who you're going to sell to, neither do I know your type of product and the position you want for it.

Notwithstanding, there are pearls in this book. Pick what you can and run with it! I have shown you some of the things that have worked for me. I didn't start wealthy, but I've built a good life for myself and my family, and I'm still on the growth curve of success. One underlying difference between myself and many of my peers who haven't made it as much as I have is the courage to get up after failing. I find it quite easy to execute now because I have failed more times than they. While I might have done 200 things and failed in 190, they've probably only tried four things and failed in all, not persisting and failing enough times to record success. Success is sometimes linked to the frequency of failure.

My charge to you is to get up and do it now. All the dots don't have to connect before you start. No successful person was fully ever ready before launching. Just dump the excuses and jump right into what must be done.

There's an interesting story in the Bible that captures my charge here. It's when Jesus said to the lepers in Luke 17:11-14, 'Go shew yourselves unto the priests.' According to the Levitical law, a leper was separated from the rest of the world and could only return when he had been healed. It was only after receiving healing that he could show himself to the priests for an examination to confirm wholeness, before returning into society. But Jesus saw these lepers and told them to show themselves to the priest, and then the Good Book records that as they were going, they became healed.

My charge to you is to get up and do it now!

That is so indicative of how businesses should be run. You may not be 100% ready but as you get up and go, you'll find solutions to the problems. You'll get healed and wholesome but first, you have to start. Go in first. Set the business plan and ensure to acquire about 60% clarity, then shoot. You'll learn on the job. Clarity sometimes comes from you already rolling in the dust of the business.

Find the needed perfection in the progress you make. Adapt—remain flexible.

By all means just start. Let the rest of the world start to hear and know what you do. Launch right now!

JUST DO IT NOW!

ABOUT THE AUTHOR

Anthony Chukwuma is a coach, trainer, public/keynote speaker, business development expert, and empowerer. He has helped multiple companies make over 20 million dollars in three to six years prior to writing this book and has established about 20 companies in the last decade.

He is a patriotic and proud Nigerian who graduated with a first-class degree from the University of Wollongong, Australia, where he majored in Computer Science. He also bagged an MBA from Southern Cross University, Australia.

With over seventeen years of working experience, Anthony has been privileged to climb the corporate ladder, starting as a customer service officer to leading sub-Saharan Africa for a multinational organisation.

He is married with three lovely kids and considers his life to be entertaining, insightful, and blessed.